Follow Me Around™
India

By Wiley Blevins

SCHOLASTIC

Content Consultant: Mary Hancock, PhD, Professor, Departments of Anthropology and History, University of California, Santa Barbara, Santa Barbara, California

Library of Congress Cataloging-in-Publication Data
Names: Blevins, Wiley, author.
Title: India / by Wiley Blevins
Description: New York : Children's Press, 2018. | Series: Follow me around | Includes index.
Identifiers: LCCN 2017038394 | ISBN 9780531234594 (library binding) | ISBN 9780531243718 (paperback)
Subjects: LCSH: India—Juvenile literature.
Classification: LCC DS407 .B653 2018 | DDC 954—dc23
LC record available at https://lccn.loc.gov/2017038394

Design: Judith Christ Lafond & Anna Tunick Tabachnik
Text: Wiley Blevins
© 2018 Scholastic Inc.

All rights reserved. Published in 2018 by Children's Press, an imprint of Scholastic Inc.
Printed in North Mankato, MN, USA 113
SCHOLASTIC, CHILDREN'S PRESS, and associated logos are trademarks and/or registered trademarks of Scholastic Inc.
Scholastic Inc., 557 Broadway, New York, NY 10012

1 2 3 4 5 6 7 8 9 10 R 27 26 25 24 23 22 21 20 19 18

Photos ©: cover background: Peter Zelei Images/Getty Images; cover child: fstop123/iStockphoto; back cover: fstop123/iStockphoto; 1: fstop123/iStockphoto; 3: RBB/Getty Images; 4 left: fstop123/iStockphoto; 6 top left: undefined undefined/iStockphoto; 6 bottom: IndiaPictures/UIG/Getty Images; 6 top right: oleandra/Shutterstock; 7 top: powerofforever/iStockphoto; 7 bottom: Adrian Pope/Getty Images; 8 left: Pradeep Gaur/Mint/Getty Images; 8 top right: Hugh Johnson/Getty Images; 8 center right top: Joe Gough/Shutterstock; 8 center right bottom: Eva Gruendemann/Shutterstock; 8 bottom right: VikramRaghuvanshi/iStockphoto; 9 top left: TerryJ/iStockphoto; 9 top center: Andrew Hounslea/Getty Images; 9 center top: lindavostrovska/iStockphoto; 9 center bottom: VeryOlive/iStockphoto; 9 bottom left: DipakShelare/iStockphoto; 9 top right: Joff Lee/Getty Images; 9 center right: Joff Lee/Getty Images; 9 bottom right: popovaphoto/iStockphoto; 10 top: Amrul Azuar Mokhtar/Shutterstock; 11 left: CRS Photo/Shutterstock; 12 bottom: Konstantin Khanzhov/Dreamstime; 12-13 background: Vadim Yerofeyev/Dreamstime; 13 top: Damayanti Learns of Nala's Virtue From a Golden Swan (chromolitho), European School, (19th century)/Private Collection/© Look and Learn/Rosenberg Collection/Bridgeman Images; 14 left: Poras Chaudhary/Getty Images; 14 top right: Svetlana Eremina/Shutterstock; 14 bottom right: Aliaksandr Mazurkevich/Dreamstime; 15 left: Meinzahn/iStockphoto; 15 right: Dariia Baranova/Shutterstock; 16 top left: aluxum/iStockphoto; 16 right: Arterra Picture Library/Alamy Images; 16 bottom: Marc Guitard/Getty Images; 17: sergwsq/iStockphoto; 18 left: James L. Stanfield/Getty Images; 18 center: Dinodia Photos/Alamy Images; 18 right: The Granger Collection; 19 left: Ann Ronan Pictures/Getty Images; 19 right: Central Press/Getty Images; 20 top: Ganesh Patil/Aanna Films/Everett Collection; 20 bottom: RBB/Getty Images; 21 top: Dinodia Photo/Getty Images; 21 bottom left: Inmagineasia/Getty Images; 21 bottom right: LAIF/Redux; 22 left: Mint Images/Art Wolfe/Getty Images; 22 right: Greg Davis/Getty Images; 23 center left top: Pacific Press/Getty Images; 23 center left bottom: Sauvik Acharyya/Shutterstock; 23 bottom left: Prakash Singh/Getty Images; 23 right: Bianca Alexis Photography (Frame made by Joan Michaels for Scholastic); 24 left: Jim Holmes/Getty Images; 24 right, 25 left: IndiaPictures/Getty Images; 25 right: Sajjad Hussain/Getty Images; 26 right: Wallace Kirkland/Getty Images; 26 left: Dinodia Photos/Alamy Images; 27 top left: Luis Davilla/Getty Images; 27 center: darrensp/iStockphoto; 27 top right: My Good Images/Shutterstock; 27 bottom: Danita Delimont/Getty Images; 28 A: RNMitra/iStockphoto; 28 B: AndreyGudkov/iStockphoto; 28 E: Mnsanthoshkumar/Dreamstime; 28 D: t-lorien/iStockphoto; 28 C: f9photos/iStockphoto; 28 F: narvikk/iStockphoto; 28 G: Dmitry Rukhlenko/Dreamstime; 30 top right: Mehmet Buma/Shutterstock; 30 top left: MargaretClavell/iStockphoto; 30 bottom: fstop123/iStockphoto.

Maps by Jim McMahon.

Table of Contents

Where in the World Is India? 4

Home Sweet Home 6

Let's Eat! 8

Off to School 10

The Golden Swan 12

Touring India 14

Our Country's History 18

It Came From India 20

Celebrate! 22

Time to Play 24

You Won't Believe This! 26

Guessing Game! 28

Preparing for Your Visit 29

The United States Compared to India ... 30

Glossary 31

Index 32

Where in the World Is India?

Namaste (nah-MUH-stay) from India! That's how we say hello. It's also how we say good-bye! I'm Harisha, your tour guide. My name means "happiness." I am happy to show you around my fascinating country.

India is a country in southern Asia. Though it is only about one-third the size of the United States, India has a lot of people! In fact, we are the second-most populated country in the world. There are many people to meet and many different places to see here. Follow me around!

Fast Facts:

- India covers 1,269,219 square miles (3,287,262 square kilometers).

- Most of India is a **peninsula** that juts out into the Indian Ocean. This land is often called the Indian subcontinent.

- The **monsoons** rule much of India's climate. The country has three basic seasons: hot and wet, hot and dry, and cool and dry.

- The Himalayas are the highest mountains in the world. They form a natural border between India and the countries to the north.

- India's longest river is the Ganges River (also known as Ganga). It is in the north.

- The scorching Thar Desert is in the western part of India.

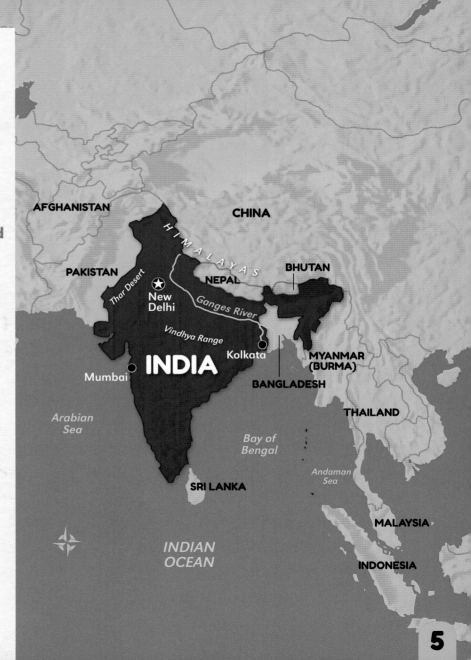

AFGHANISTAN

CHINA

PAKISTAN

HIMALAYAS

BHUTAN

NEPAL

Thar Desert

New Delhi

Ganges River

Vindhya Range

Kolkata

MYANMAR (BURMA)

Mumbai

INDIA

BANGLADESH

THAILAND

Arabian Sea

Bay of Bengal

Andaman Sea

SRI LANKA

MALAYSIA

INDIAN OCEAN

INDONESIA

Houses in Delhi

Country homes are usually made of mud, with thatched roofs.

Home Sweet Home

I am from New Delhi, India. Families in India, including mine, are often large. Visit my home and meet my parents, grandparents, two brothers, two sisters, an aunt, an uncle, and three cousins. We all share chores around the house. For example, my mother and I visit an outdoor market each week to buy fresh fruits and vegetables.

Rangoli

Outside the entrance to my home is a *rangoli*. This is a colorful design made on the floor with rice, flour, sand, and other materials to welcome visitors. Some traditional rangoli designs are hundreds of years old. My mother taught me how to make several of them. These designs are usually passed down from mother to daughter.

Chula

About 71 percent of people in India live in the country. Country homes are usually small and simple. You'll find very little furniture, and a simple mat might be used for sleeping. Cooking is done on a small clay stove called a *chula*. It is usually in one corner of a main room or in a small separate room.

Many villages have shared areas, including lands where animals graze, water wells, and places for worship. Most villagers farm. They grow peanuts, rice, tea, cotton, potatoes, and wheat. Some also raise sheep, goats, and chickens. I love visiting my relatives in the country. We go fishing and play outdoors all day.

Religions in India

People follow many different religions in India. The two most common are Hinduism and Islam. Some Indians are Christian. Buddhists and Jains follow religions that originated in India thousands of years ago. Sikhism began here about 500 years ago.

Praying

Chutney

Curries

Let's Eat!

Each region in India has its own special food. Ingredients depend on what is grown or caught there. But wherever you visit, you'll taste curry! This spicy, creamy sauce is used in both vegetable and meat dishes. Yum! We also use a lot of *chutney*, a delicious **condiment**.

We don't usually eat with a fork or spoon. People in northern India often scoop up food with flatbreads such as *naan*. In the south, rice is mixed with the food and eaten with your fingers.

Chai, or tea, is a popular drink, especially in northern India. It often has milk, sugar, and spices in it. Coffee is common farther south, where coffee grows. A cold drink I love is *lassi*. It is made from yogurt or buttermilk. It often has rose or mango flavors mixed in.

Lassi

Naan

Street food

When you're roaming our city streets, stop by one of our food stalls and grab some tasty chaat, or snacks. My favorite snack is *bhel puri*. It's a mix of puffed rice, chickpeas, onions, tomatoes, and green peppers. You have to try it!

Indian cooking is known for its spices. A spice mixture ground into a paste or powder is called masala. The seven most common spices included in masalas are cardamom, cumin, cayenne pepper, ginger, cinnamon, turmeric, and coriander. These spices add loads of flavor to our dishes.

My family and I do not eat meat. My family practices the Hindu religion. Hindus believe in respect for all living things. As a result, many Hindus, including us, are vegetarians.

Spices From India

Cardamom

Cumin

Cayenne pepper

Ginger

Cinnamon

Turmeric

Coriander

India has one of the largest school systems in the world.

Off to School

In India, public school is free until we are 14 years old. To continue school after that, we must pay **tuition** and buy our books and uniforms. Unfortunately, this is very expensive. Many of my friends will quit school to work. Not all kids graduate from secondary school, and most graduates are boys. I hope to become a teacher to help the girls in my neighborhood continue their studies.

There are more than 50 kids in my class. Luckily, I get to sit next to my best *dost (DOHST)*, or friend. We wear uniforms to school, which I quite like. Instead of earning letter grades like in the United States, we are given numbers from 1 through 10. A 10 is considered "outstanding." I work hard to earn good grades!

दोस्त
(dost)
friend

Lunch at my school is free. We always sit down on the floor to eat it!

One of the main things we learn in school is how to read and write Hindi. Hindi uses the same alphabet as the ancient Sanskrit language. We also study English. Kids in many regions study their local language, too. As many as 461 different languages and dialects are spoken here.

In school, we read a lot of traditional tales. One of my favorites is the story of the princess Savitri. Savitri loved her husband so much that the strength of her love saved him from death. Other stories, such as "The Golden Swan," teach lessons.

How to Count in Hindi

Knowing how to count to 10 is important when you visit India. Also, pay attention to how the numbers are written.

1	१	(eyk)
2	२	(doh)
3	३	(teen)
4	४	(chahr)
5	५	(pahnch)
6	६	(chah)
7	७	(saht)
8	८	(ahrt)
9	९	(nau)
10	१०	(dahs)

The Golden Swan

Once upon a time, there lived a swan with beautiful golden feathers. The swan lived in a pond near the home of a poor woman and her two daughters. Each day, the swan watched as the woman and her daughters struggled. They never had enough food. Their clothes were tattered. Their home stood withered and ready to fall down.

"I must help this poor family," thought the swan. "I will give them one of my golden feathers. The woman can sell it and buy all that she needs."

The woman was overjoyed by the generous gift. "We can now live in comfort," she cried. "Thank you! Thank you!" said the two daughters.

Time passed. The swan continued to give the woman and her daughters one golden feather whenever they needed it. But one day, the woman became greedy. She turned to her daughters and said, "I do not trust that swan. She might fly away and never return. We will be poor again. The next time she comes, I will take all her feathers."

"Don't do this," cried the daughters. "The swan will be hurt, or worse." But the woman ignored them. The next time that the swan returned, the woman grabbed her and plucked all the bird's golden feathers.

Angry, the swan turned her golden feathers into worthless chicken feathers. "I wanted to help you," honked the swan. "But you wanted to kill me. You will never see me again." And as the swan flew away, she squawked, "This is what happens to those who are greedy!"

A street in Old Delhi

Lodi Gardens

Spice market

Touring India

New Delhi: Capital City

Welcome to my city, New Delhi. It's the capital of India. It is located inside Delhi, a **megacity** with more than 22 million people. Delhi includes New Delhi, where I live, and Old Delhi. So, we're a city within a city! When you visit, the first thing you'll notice is how crowded it is. Beep! Beep! Buses, motorcycles, cows, and people selling things fill our streets. Don't worry! One fun way to get around is by *rickshaw*. Hop in this old-fashioned cart with a friend and relax as the driver pedals through the busy streets. I recommend riding in a rickshaw around the historic streets of Old Delhi and stopping at one of the many spice markets.

If the crowds are too much for you, hop on the Metro. You can zoom around my city safely and quickly on this **subway** system. The trains run every 8 to 12 minutes. Our subway system has six train lines and 135 stations, so you can reach most places you will want to visit. Make sure you stop by Lodi Gardens. This park is in New Delhi, but it's full of ancient buildings.

I Love Yoga

Yoga began in India and is now popular all over the world. I do yoga every week. The word *yoga* comes from an ancient Sanskrit word meaning "unite." Yoga is more of a religious experience than an exercise for us. We unite our minds and bodies with the world around us. This involves both **meditation** and movement. Try some of these yoga poses at home. You might one day become a yogi!

Cat

Tree

Cow

Warrior one

Downward facing dog

Extended boat

Varanasi ghats

Bandhavgarh National Park

Beyond the Megacities

Delhi, Mumbai, and Kolkata are cities with more than 10 million people each. Varanasi is a much smaller city, but equally interesting. There, you should visit the banks of the Ganges River. The town has dozens of stairways called ghats leading down to the water, where people can bathe and worship. But if you really need a break from the hustle and bustle, head north to the Himalayas. This astonishing mountain range has many of Earth's highest peaks. Bird-watchers should visit Keoladeo Ghana National Park. More than 50 different species of birds can be seen in only a few hours. But my favorite activity is trekking by elephant through the Bandhavgarh National Park. Visitors ride on special seats on an elephant's back. The seats can hold several people at once, so groups can go exploring together!

Keep an eye out for our many palace hotels. These old palaces can be interesting and beautiful places to stay. But they are quite pricey!

The Taj Mahal is considered one of the Seven Wonders of the Modern World.

Other Fun Places to Visit

Travel to the city of Agra and you'll spot India's most famous and photographed building: the Taj Mahal. It is a huge **tomb** made of white marble. Precious stones and gems fill its walls. Wow! Around it you'll find beautiful gardens and fountains. Shah Jahan, an Indian ruler in the 1600s, built it for his wife, Mumtaz Mahal. She died while giving birth to her 14th child. The shah was so sad, he ordered 20,000 workers using hundreds of elephants to build this monument. It took more than 20 years to complete. Today, two to four million people visit the Taj Mahal every year. You have to take a picture there!

Our Country's History

We are proud of our country's long history. People have lived in what is now India for thousands of years. One of the world's oldest civilizations formed in the Indus Valley here. Most of this region lies in what is now Pakistan. The Indus Valley civilization built great cities out of brick and stone. For centuries, India had many different kingdoms and rulers. One of the longest ruling empires was the more than 300-year-long Mughal dynasty, when Muslim rulers reigned. Great pieces of art and architecture were created during this time.

Timeline: India's History

Mohenjo Daro

2600 BCE

First cities
Cities such as Lothal and Mohenjo Daro develop along the Indus River.

Sanskrit

1700 BCE

Indo-Aryan language speakers
People from central Asia migrate into India. Their language develops into Sanskrit.

1000–1857 CE

Mongol and Turkic invasions and Mughal Empire
Mongol and Turkic armies invade. They introduce Islam into India. By the 1500s, they start the Mughal dynasty.

In the 1500s, India began trading with European countries such as Portugal and Great Britain. Slowly, these countries began taking more control. Eventually, the British took over and ruled for 350 years. This had a great affect on how we lived. We began speaking English. Our buildings, schools, and clothing began to mirror those in Great Britain. It wasn't until 1947 that India became independent. As part of the agreement, the land was divided into two countries: Pakistan (where many Muslims now live) and India (where most Hindus now live).

Queen Victoria

Mohandas Gandhi

1500s–1947

British rule

European powers invade. India officially becomes a British colony in 1858. Queen Victoria is named empress of India in 1877.

1885–1947

Struggle against Great Britain

Leaders such as Mohandas Gandhi and Jawaharlal Nehru organize peaceful protests against British rule.

1947

Independence

The Indian region gains independence from Great Britain and is split in two. Pakistan and India form and write their own constitutions, or sets of laws.

It Came From India

India makes more than 800 movies a year—more than any other country in the world! Mumbai is the heart of Bollywood filmmaking. Bollywood gets its name from "Bombay," an old name for Mumbai. Bombay + Hollywood = Bollywood! Bollywood movies are often filled with songs and dances, which help tell the stories. If you haven't seen one yet, give these films a try!

Traditional Indian dances tell stories, too, but in a different way. The dancers use hand gestures and special movements. These dances started as part of religious ceremonies long ago. Now, you can see them everywhere. I love the dancers' beautiful makeup and costumes.

Maharaja is an ancient name for rulers in India. It became a common title in my country in the 1850s. Though Britain controlled India, some areas had their own local kings. These maharajahs were famous for their lavish lifestyles. They lived in palaces, wore expensive clothes, and took part in rituals and parades.

I dress much like you do in the United States. My mother, however, likes to wear a silk sari made from one piece of cloth 15 to 21 feet (4.6 to 6.4 meters) long. At formal events, my father sometimes wears *kurta-pajamas*. The *kurta* is a long, loose-fitting shirt. The *pajama* is pants made of light cloth. Men also wear *dhoti* and *lungi*, which wrap around the waist.

A section of the city of Hyderabad is called Cyberabad. It is chock-full of high-tech companies. It represents the growing technology world that is sweeping India. Because of our high-tech growth, India has more new millionaires each year than any other country.

Diwali celebrates the triumph of good over evil.

Kumbh Mela

Celebrate!

Everyone loves a holiday, and we have some fun ones in India. Diwali is my favorite. It's known as the Hindu festival of lights, and it lasts five days! We place candles called *diyas* around our home. Diyas are saucers filled with oil and a cotton wick. My friends and I once took a special trip to put a diya in the Ganges River. We made a wish as our diya floated away. According to tradition, if it stays lit until we can no longer see it, our wish could come true!

If you are lucky, you might catch Kumbh Mela. This huge religious festival takes place every three years. Hindus go to one of four different sites along certain rivers and bathe in the **sacred** waters. So many people gather that we have set world records!

Other Fun Celebrations

February March

Holi (Festival of Color)
Grab a handful of colored water and powder, and throw it at your family and friends. That's how we honor the god Krishna!

April

Vaisakhi
People wear colorful clothes, share food, and play and dance to music to mark the Sikh New Year. Many Sikhs also attend religious ceremonies.

August 15

Independence Day
Every August, we celebrate our independence from British rule. Enjoy the colorful costumes, music, dancing, and parades.

Eid al-Fitr
This holiday marks the end of Ramadan, a Muslim holy month. Muslims pray, eat, and exchange gifts. Eid al-Fitr happens at different times each year.

Make an Indian Mirror

Materials: scissors, colorful cardboard, 6 x 6-inch mirror tile, pencil, paintbrush, glue, gold paper, glitter, stickers, double-sided tape, hook

Ask an adult to help!

Directions:

1 **Cut** the colorful cardboard into a square the same size as the mirror tile.

2 In the middle of the cardboard, **draw** a curved arch that comes to a point at the top. Leave plenty of room around the arch to decorate. **Cut** out the arch. The frame is what's left.

3 **Paint** glue over the frame's front.

4 **Decorate.** For example, cut out an elephant or lotus flower from gold paper and place it on the frame. Sprinkle glitter all over the frame. Add shiny stickers.

5 **Tape** the frame to the mirror tile.

6 **Attach** a hook securely to the back of the tile. Then **hang** the mirror in your bedroom.

Cricket

There are plenty of beautiful views for hikers and climbers in the Himalayas.

Time to Play

Cricket, field hockey (our national game), and soccer are especially popular sports here. Cricket is sort of like baseball. We use a ball, bats, and low stands called wickets. We first learned this sport from the British. Today, you'll find people playing it all across India—from big cities to small villages. When India's national cricket team plays on TV, millions of us gather to watch. And we have a lot to cheer about. Our "Boys in Blue" are among the highest ranked national teams in the world!

Hiking, horseback riding, and fishing are also common. These are great ways to explore India outside the city, from the high mountains to the low streams.

Chess

My friends and I also like to play chess. This board game was invented in my country more than 1,500 year ago. Another board game I love is snakes and ladders.

A fun traditional game my friends and I play is *uffangali*. Its name comes from two words: *gali*, meaning "wind," and *uff*, meaning "blowing." It can be played on any floor. Give it a try!

1 Pile up a few handfuls of seeds or small candies on the floor.

2 Each player takes a turn. The player takes a deep breath and blows as hard as he or she can. But only once!

3 The player collects any seeds or candies blown off the pile. Be careful! Each seed or candy must be picked up without touching any nearby seeds or candies. A player who moves other seeds or candies loses a turn.

4 The game ends when all the seeds or candies have been picked up. The player with the biggest pile wins.

You Won't Believe This!

Mohandas Gandhi is known as Mahatma (great soul, or saint). He lived very simply and had few pieces of furniture. He led a nonviolent protest against British rule in India. It helped lead to my country's independence. That's why we call him the father of the nation.

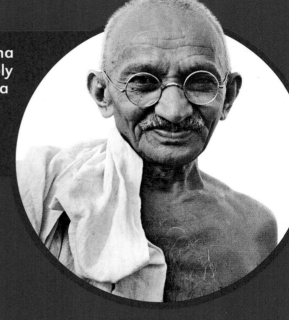

Many cows wander the streets of India. Hindus believe that cows are special animals, so we don't kill them for food. Each cow's head is marked with a *tilak*, a Hindu symbol for good fortune. On a holiday called Gopastami, we decorate the cows with flowers and ribbons.

The Himalayan Mountains are high, rugged, and beautiful. The name *Himalaya* comes from two Sanskrit words: *hima*, meaning "snow," and *alaya*, meaning "home." And due to the movements of the **plates** that make up Earth's crust, the mountains grow taller every year!

Saffron, called *kesar* in India, is a popular and yummy spice. It comes from the crocus flower. Surprisingly, it takes 165,000 crocus flowers to make only about 2 pounds (1 kilogram) of saffron. As a result, it is the most expensive spice in the world!

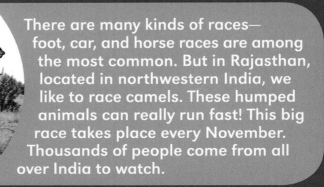

There are many kinds of races— foot, car, and horse races are among the most common. But in Rajasthan, located in northwestern India, we like to race camels. These humped animals can really run fast! This big race takes place every November. Thousands of people come from all over India to watch.

Guessing Game!

Here are some other great sites around India. If you have time, try to see them all!

1. Jog Falls
2. Gwalior Fort
3. Golden Temple
4. Gajner wildlife sanctuary
5. Jama Masjid mosque
6. Red Fort
7. Calcutta Botanic Garden banyan

A

This banyan, located in a beautiful botanic garden, is a type of tree that sends down roots from its branches. Each root becomes another "trunk." It has enough roots to look like a whole forest!

B

This is one of more than 100 wildlife sanctuaries dedicated to saving our unique wildlife.

C

This temple is the holiest site in the Sikh religion. It is famous for the gold that decorates the outside of its walls.

D

This palace fort, with its dark-red walls, was built by Mughal emperor Shah Jahan starting in 1639. It is now a symbol of India's independence.

This is among the most famous waterfalls in India. So beautiful!

E

F

This is one of India's most famous mosques, or Muslim places of worship. The mosque's entrance faces west toward Mecca, Saudi Arabia, Islam's holiest city.

This fort is built high on a large sandstone bluff and is one of the most impressive structures in India.

G

Answer Key
1E, 2G, 3C, 4B, 5F, 6D, 7A

Preparing for Your Visit

By now, you should be ready to hop on a plane to India. Here are some tips to prepare for your trip.

1 Before you come to India, exchange your money. Our money is called rupees. Each rupee equals 100 paise. You'll need rupees to buy fun **souvenirs**.

2 It's best to not drink the local tap water. Your body is not used to the water in other countries, so it can make you sick. Instead, buy bottled water—even for brushing your teeth. And remember, ice cubes are made of water!

3 You might have difficulty finding the kind of bathrooms you're used to in the United States. Many toilets here are set into the floor. To use one, you squat over it. Carry a roll of toilet paper and some antiseptic wipes just in case.

4 If you're feeling adventurous, stay in one of our wildlife sanctuaries or national parks. Take a hat, binoculars, and a camera. But don't wear bright colors. They attract unwanted attention from the animals.

5 If you are traveling by train and your ticket says "wait list" or "WL," be warned. You probably won't get a seat. It's best to make other travel plans.

6 We have many religious sites in India. Remember to take off your shoes before entering. In mosques, you must cover your head, arms, and legs. No shorts or tank tops, either.

7 In India, the left hand and foot are considered unclean. Never touch something in a temple or eat with your left hand. You might want to practice at home first.

The United States Compared to India

Official Name	United States of America (USA)	Republic of India
Official Language	No official language, though English is most commonly used	Hindi (English is also widely spoken)
Population	325 million	More than 1.3 billion
Flag		
Money	Dollar	Rupee
Location	North America	Asia
Highest Point	Denali (Mount McKinley)	Kangchenjunga (third-highest mountain in the world)
Lowest Point	Death Valley	Kuttanad
Size	World's third-largest country	About one-third the size of the United States
National Anthem	"The Star-Spangled Banner"	"Jana Gana Mana"

So now you know some important and fascinating things about my country, India. I hope to see you someday riding a rickshaw through one of our city streets, hiking high in the Himalayas, or enjoying a tasty meal with curry and tea. Until then . . . *namaste*. Good-bye.

Glossary

condiment
(KAHN-duh-muhnt)
something used to enhance
the flavor of food

meditation
(med-uh-TAY-shuhn)
the act of thinking deeply
and quietly as a way of
relaxing the mind and body

megacity
(MEG-uh-sih-tee)
a very large city, or an
area that includes several
large cities

monsoons
(mahn-SOONZ)
rainy seasons brought
on by very strong winds
blowing in from the ocean

peninsula
(puh-NIN-suh-luh)
a piece of land that sticks
out from a larger landmass
and is almost completely
surrounded by water

plates *(PLAYTS)*
the large pieces into which
Earth's crust is divided

sacred *(SAY-krid)*
holy, or having to do
with religion

souvenirs
(soo-vuh-NEERZ)
objects that are kept as
a reminder of a place,
person, or something
that happened

subway *(SUHB-way)*
having to do with a
system of trains that runs
underground in a city

tomb *(TOOM)*
a grave, room, or building
for holding a dead body

tuition *(too-ISH-uhn)*
money paid to a college or
private school for a student
to study there

Index

animals, 7, 26, 27, 28, 29
cities, 9, 14–15, 16, 17, 18, 21
clothes, 19, 21, 23, 29
food, 7, 8–9, 23, 26, 27

games, 24, 25, 27
history, 18–19, 26
holidays, 22–23, 26
homes, 6, 7, 22
land, 4–5, 19, 27, 30

languages, 4, 11, 18, 30
money, 29, 30
religions, 7, 9, 20, 26, 28, 29
schools, 10–11, 19

Facts for Now

Visit this Scholastic website for more information on India and to download the Teaching Guide for this series:

www.factsfornow.scholastic.com   Enter the keyword **India**

About the Author

Wiley Blevins lives and works in New York City. His greatest love is traveling, and he has been all over the world. He has written several books for children, including the Ick and Crud series and the Scary Tales Retold series.